THE BIG BOOK
OF
REAL FIRE ENGINES

THE BIG BOOK

OF REAL

FIRE

Text by ELIZABETH CAMERON
Illustrations by GEORGE J. ZAFFO

Technical advice by Fire Commissioner J. FRANK HAND and Fire Chief EDWARD GALL, SR.
Mount Vernon Fire Department, Mount Vernon, New York

ENGINES

GROSSET & DUNLAP · Publishers
NEW YORK

ISBN: 0-448-02141-2 (Trade Edition)   ISBN: 0-448-03689-4 (Library Edition)

Copyright, 1950, by Grosset & Dunlap, Inc. © 1958, by Grosset & Dunlap, Inc.

All rights reserved under International and Pan-American Copyright Conventions.

Published simultaneously in Canada.   Printed in the United States of America.

1976 PRINTING

This big truck is a new kind of hook-and-ladder. It is easy to drive. It can turn in a narrow street. Look at the ladders. They are 65 to 100 feet long. They reach to high places.

Do you see the open cab in front of the truck? The driver sits in the open cab. He can see all around him. He can tell how much room he has to turn the truck.

The airport fire truck has a big water tank. It holds a lot of water.
The firemen on the truck can put out a fire in any part of the airport.
They use water from the big tank.

Some airport firemen use foam on the fire. The foam covers the
fire. The airport truck carries many things to put out the fire. The truck
is always ready to go to a fire.

The pumper pumps water. It pumps it from the hydrant. The pumper makes the water go faster through the hoses.

This fire engine can be used in any kind of weather. It is used mostly in cold weather. Five men can sit in the closed cab. In cold weather the men are warm in the closed cab.

Do you see the large round outlet at the side of the truck? This is for the black hose. One end of the hose goes into the outlet. One end goes to the hydrant.

Do you see the two narrow water outlets above the large round one? These outlets are for white canvas hoses.

This pumper has an open cab. It is used mostly in warm weather. This pumper is very big. It pumps water much faster than the smaller pumper. A 14-foot ladder hangs on the side.

Do you see the outlets for the hoses? There are outlets on both sides of the truck. The firemen use the outlets on the side of the truck that is nearest to the hydrant.

A NIGHT WITH A

Night firemen have a large room in the firehouse. They sleep at home during the day. They stay in the firehouse at night. They are always ready to go to a fire.

1 At 6 o'clock in the evening the night fireman comes to the firehouse.

2 He lines up with other firemen to show that he is ready. He is told what to do.

5 The fireman runs to the pole as soon as he hears the bell. He slides down the pole. This is a quick way to get downstairs.

6 The fireman puts on his fire clothes in a hurry. He is ready to go to the fire.

9 Soon the fire is out. The fire chief calls out, "Shut down. Pick up. Go back to the firehouse." The firemen go back.

10 At the firehouse the firemen take off the used hose. They put on clean hose. They clean the fire engine.

13 The wet hose is hung in the drying room. The hose is long. Some hose is 50 feet long.

FIREMAN ON DUTY

3 The fireman goes upstairs. He changes into his working clothes.

4 A man turns in an alarm at a firebox. A bell rings in the fireman's room.

7 The fireman runs to the fire engine. Away he goes to the fire.

8 The firemen pull out the hose. They hook the pumper to the hydrant. They put water on the fire.

11 Soon the engine is clean. The fireman says, "The engine is ready to go to another fire."

12 Other firemen clean the used hose. They get it ready for the drying room.

14 At 8 o'clock the next morning the night fireman leaves the firehouse. He goes home to sleep. The day fireman takes his place at the firehouse.

Zeffo

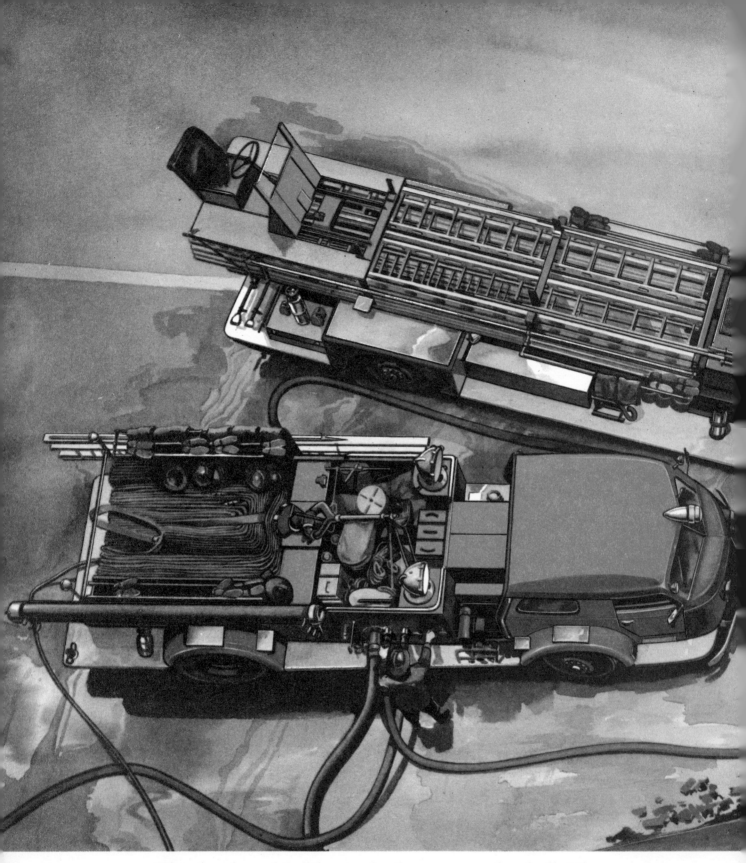

This hook-and-ladder is the biggest truck of all. This truck goes out on big fires. A fireman sits in front and drives the truck. A fireman sits in the back of the hook-and-ladder. He steers the rear wheels. The two firemen work together to drive the hook-and-ladder.

Do you see the ladders? They can go up and down. They stop
going up when the ladder touches the building.

The hook-and-ladder does not carry any hose. A pumper goes
with the hook-and-ladder to carry the hose.

This fire engine is a hose truck. It goes out on all the fire alarms. Sometimes it goes with a hook-and-ladder. Sometimes it goes with a pumper. Sometimes it goes alone.

This fire engine carries hose on a reel. The hose goes to the 100-gallon tank of water. The hose truck also carries a first-aid box. This fire engine is a very useful one.

This truck is used in the country. The truck carries its own water in a big tank. It has two pumps on the front of the truck. It has many feet of canvas hose.

Look at the wheels on this fire engine. The back set of each group
drives the truck. The truck can go over bumpy roads. It can go through
fields where there are no roads.

THE FIRE ALARM

Follow the red arrows and see how it works.

1 FIREBOX (Closed)

This is the way a fire alarm box looks on a pole. The number of this firebox is 3226.

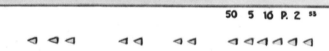

3 RECORDER TAPE

This is the fire alarm recorder tape. The marks tell the number of the firebox. The time and the date are on the tape, too.

5 BELL

The bell will ring at a firehouse. It will ring at the firehouse that is nearest to firebox 3226.

SYSTEM

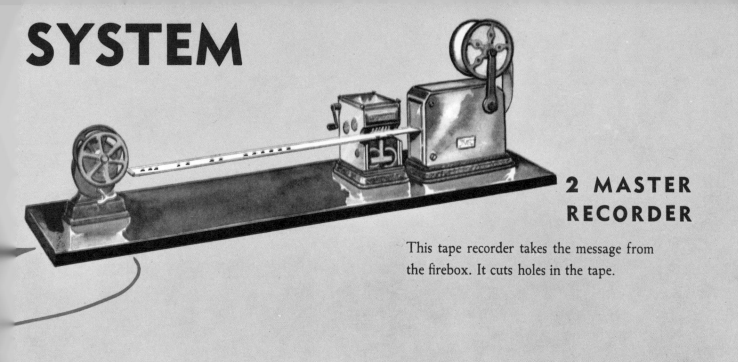

2 MASTER RECORDER

This tape recorder takes the message from the firebox. It cuts holes in the tape.

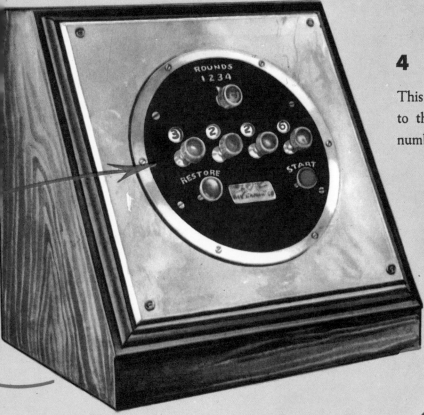

4 MANUAL TRANSMITTER

This transmitter sends the messages to the firehouses. It sends out the number of the box.

6 FIREBOX (Open)

The firemen go to the box. The person who sent the alarm should wait at the box. He should be there to tell the firemen where to go.

Zaffo

This truck is a kitchen on wheels. It goes to the fires with the fire engines. It carries food for the firemen. It goes out on large fires.

The field kitchen truck parks close to the fire. It does not get in the way of the firemen. This field kitchen truck is used in big cities.

The Fire Chief has a red car. He uses the car to hurry to all the fires. The siren makes a loud noise. Then all the other cars stop.

Sometimes the Fire Chief does not drive fast. He does not use the siren. His red car goes along with the other cars on the street.

This is a very big fire. It is a general alarm fire. Many trucks go to a general alarm fire.

Firemen work fast to save the buildings. They work hard so the fire does not spread.

They use many hoses to get water to put out the fire.

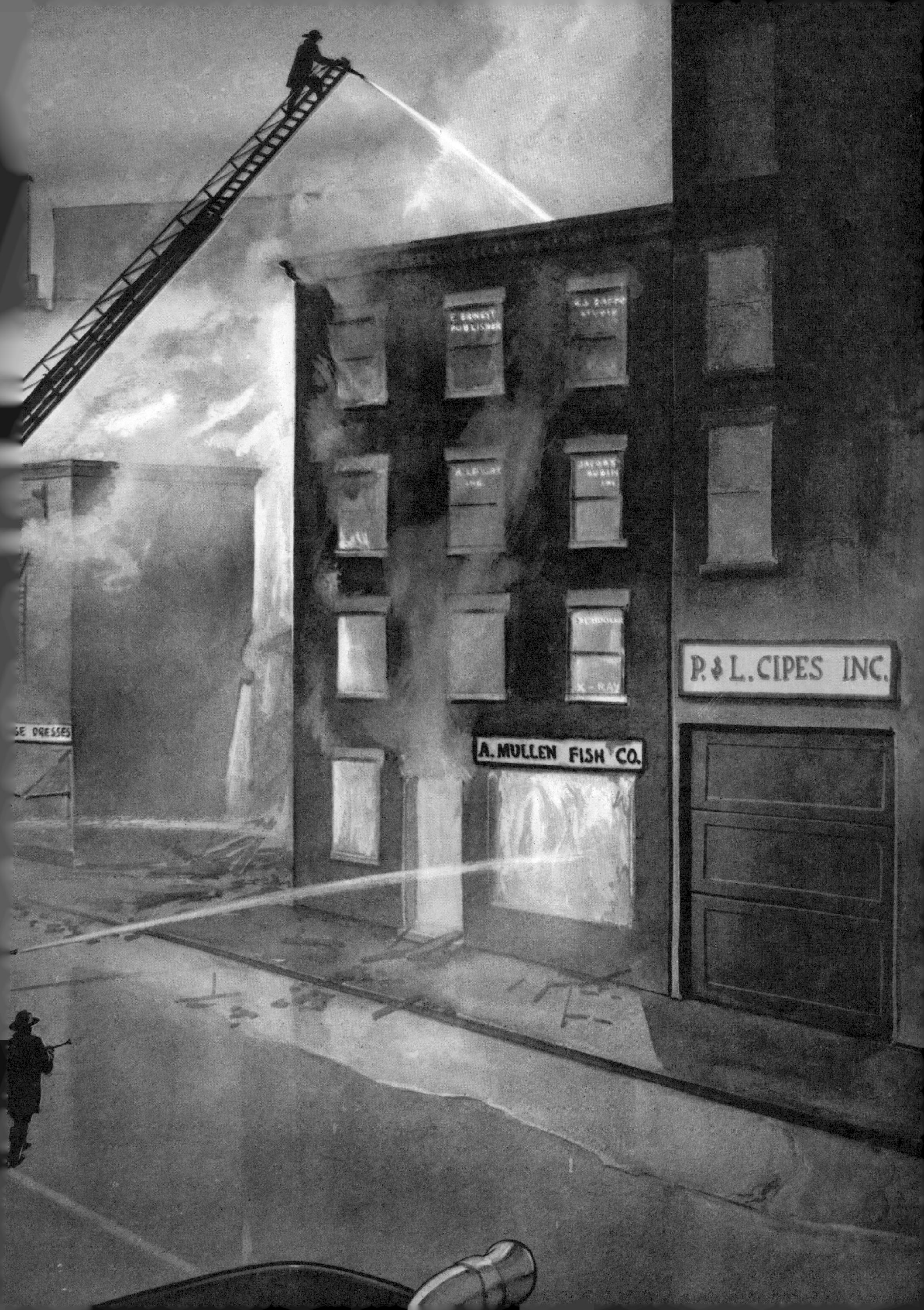

E. ERNEST
PUBLISHER
X-RAY
A. MULLEN FISH CO.
P. & L. CIPES INC.